LYRICAL CARTOGRAPHY

A Collection of Poems

BRIAN PATRICK CROFT

For My Mother and Father,
K.M.,
and
Those for Whom a Need is Present

Table of Contents

I.

The mind is as a vivarium;
verdant, self-oxygenated, and ever-growing–
but seemingly with a similar ambivalence
for the material from which its seedlings rise.

"Truth"

Everyone needs to hear the words, and so we must, too, say them:
How it's ok, even when it clearly isn't–
That we are doing a good job, even when we aren't–
How we are kind, strong, thoughtful when we're selfish or weak–
That everything will be well, even if no one knows for certain.

We are liars.

But here we lie for others, not ourselves, and they for us–
thus, in doing so,
we make the words true.

"Body of Knowledge"

The Self is Academy, to be held in esteem
as much as any cloistered walls of ivory, candle-lit,
any library, aged but verdant in its illuminated leaves and lines from poets and
philosophers,
or hallowed university of marbled floors imprinted with the steps of the
virginal and the wise.
It is our house, our bark, our mirror, and our lens, and in ourselves
the Disciplines present, if one but reposes in reflection.

Of illusion and of matter is the mind, both wonderful and wondering;
unperceiving when broken, unruly,
unkind to its Atlas below in times of anxiety and doubt;
it is both the observer of the universe
and that celestial entity itself.
Its omnipotence reveals its paradigmatic paradox: we command that which we
never want to be submissive, wishing to restrain it when we please, yet
allowing it strength and independence to create, to solve, to salve.
A machine inexplicable by the structure in which it lives, yet functioning
despite our ignorance:
Opening, closing, shunting–"Yes" or "No" to all directives it itself gives to
animate the whole, generating the slightest of whims and severe impetuses,
decisions moral or mechanical,
–whether to act, why thus and thus is true, what should live–
and behaviors malignant and benign.
Yet the psyche and its driver, in our most desperate moments of crying
"Why?" allows us, somehow, to find contentment, even if through simple
memory or foolish fancy;
and in its uncertain certainty we alter all–
see the fact, yet let it waver,
find insupportable belief, and let it reign,
and accept only what we–or it–so choose, reality bending from its heft.

But if it is obscure to us, all but inscrutable is it to others—
and so upon its shell is borne our distinct aspect, a simulacrutive expression
which, though unique, somehow mirrors that of every other of our kind.
And while, as wrote the Bard, there is "no art to find the mind's construction
in the face," if one were to denude all of what one is, it would be through eyes
entrancing, the bitten lip, pulsing temples, brows declined.
The infant, while sounds have waved through amniotic walls before its
crowning, sees its own reflection when it finds the light: a parent's face, more
communicative
than any language mouthed or penned.
A smile peals, tears—of joy or sorrow—narrate an ongoing story,
cheeks gaunt an epic sing. Even senses seem to fail in faces,
with prickles on the neck at eyes behind that we can somehow feel, their
power to embolden or burst the heart undeniable.
The faltering voice of boy or girl is cast aside when, on playground carved
from aging, concreted city, two pairs of tracking eyes discover the kiss—
the wingbeat of a butterfly in time, and just as rousing. Perhaps in later years,
as tongues master other lessons, one may know that all the syntactical
stratagems of poems, subtlety of texts, or fervency of oratory will,
when eyelids close and open with those of a lover laying close,
appear superfluous.

An intimate navigation of the core, the torso, exemplifies true geography––past
Ptolemy, beyond Cabot and Columbus, Cabral and Vespucci, to regions fit for
exploration.
Below neck lithe or stout, laid out before as are hillocks, meadows,
and vales to able pioneer,
the skin beckons;
its longitude intoxicating, but only less so than its spread, with mounded
pectorals or supple breasts. Such virile constitution secretes heat, anticipation
visible in tremoring obliques, and all quakes as the heart encased—the
Animator-liberates, pheromones hovering now on sweating plains,
and blurring eyes
lose themselves in this seductive topography for which we need no compass.
Senses aggregate to overwhelm orientation as darker and unsounded regions,

which no words can properly depict,

await discovery-yet even as the sensual abates, the form intoxicates, its

workings hidden: Lay the head upon the bosom and hear that heart,

now regimented, imagine arteries, veins, flows to the iliacs;

lungs in regulation now, oxygenation tuned to altitudes miles about the seas,

and retentive of brief life under those same waters-a trunk most viable. It is

easy to ascribe to this the soul, the guide for us to that "undiscovered country"

to which there is no route, no bearing-and so, too, is it easy to throw such

thoughts aside and simply wander the terrain, mapping the elevations and

declivities until we set the work aside,

at peace amongst the hachures.

Topology ends not with the continental body, nor does Vitruvian Man his

equilibrium find from a single point: Sweeping limbs, parallels set

upon their axes manifest Nature's balance and the circumferential reach of

human hands,

those brutes that tear and choke and yet are delicate enough to soothe the

cheek, pluck an errant lash from out the eye. Equal sets on left and right, angles

matching angles, nimble digits at their endpoints;

while sets of symbols from mind to paper channel through, it is by these we

measure, plot the line to see its slope, demonstrate the orders in infinity.

Children count upon their fingers,

grasping the easy simplification of the complex,

and later wield their manipulative power to create upon the earth worlds of

their own-

much as a watchmaker teases jeweled gears into a case of gold, then animates

the whole, radii and weight and diameter harnessed to reflect the rotation of

the cosmos, to control it through a crown between our fingers,

and in that ticking animation find that although numbers will continue,

our enumeration ceases-the calculus of human life beyond our skill to learn.

As distinct as are our fingerprints, we walk distinguishable yet fitted to our life's

velocity, our silhouette unique, and move from measured, pensive steps to

bold and thoughtless sprints to destinations unseen, unknown,

as driven by the heart.

Bipedal animation: pulleys greased and levers thickened,
enabling us to flee, or stand our ground in violence,
impotently pace as loved ones absent or in suffering bring unmanageable
energy, us weakening in adverse anticipation,
or remain static as the mind slips on glazed subjects, footholds not to be found.
All have felt a restlessness of mind, of soul, and so we walk,
counting on the physical to physic that inside.
Potential to kinetic, all at force of thought. Femoral muscles and tendons and
their fibrous elasticity, pushing us past competitors of our biome,
grant stability on earth and such less-solid stuff on which we find ourselves,
and profound is the loss of their support in later years,
gravitation irresistible. Yet, while they can, all else they raise,
in some evolutionary triumph, distancing the viscera,
the mind-our softer, yielding parts-from roads of peril and the calling dust,
and diminish the space between the each of us.

And the form itself, in its way parchment-covered, shows its history;
events of decay and of growth,
scars gained through foolishness and societal fracture,
encounters with Nature and Time, apparent in hair, whether stripped or baked
under countless suns, with colors expressive, lustrous, ripe.
Like a winter count
or unfurled scroll from a forgotten hollow, our memories and passions,
our losses and dashed hopes
are pictorialized upon us always, in eyes, blemishes, creases, clefts in the softest
flesh, pock-marks and liver-spots, callouses from the work of life,
in pregnant lips of red and blushing cheeks.
The frame itself, too, swells or bends from its encounters, its physical toils
in gymnasiums, fields, quarries-we, the agitators of stone-
and backs are bent behind oak or plywood desks in labor of a different kind.
And while we shield-or spectacle-ourselves in the
raiment *du jour*, the gay colors of avian cousins, flowing dresses that harness air
or overworn, familiar denim,
we simply layer our story in doing so, exposing further
all that we have learned during our hours in both the darkness and light.

So is our clay set for the sculptor, with only "Life" to add-the
Obscure Engine, immaterial, the final touch of the unseen Artist.
Joined, molded, and patterned, with incising, if not precise, of purpose-
meaningful and measured to each "I," so that even the
most base of us is worthy of inclusion into statuary, our
bodies shaped into images as relevant and beautiful as any Master's oil,
as just as fragile. The simplest details become us, and
that which may be met with self-disgust, a single flaw, refines the whole.
Each birth is Renaissance,
each human figure a potentiality,
each a Designer in itself to mold and model its own world-
or to desiccate through ignorance and hate, then fissuring itself to pieces.
We are the medium through which the Truth is told, our singular realties less
varied than we know, though each of different hue.
And if, indeed, it is Time and Trial that lifted us from out the waters,
no hand of deity having set our kind upon a wheel,
still are we remarkable, deserving of study and of sanctification,
as likely to engender the emotions as any example of our Art.

And so most instructive is the body, that ephemeral and only, at once
our school and home-
and no sage, no rector of podium or pulpit
can impart knowledge as can the intimacy of skin, the work of hands and
active limbs,
a countenance enlightened, the sounding of a mind,
or the stirring exploration of the Self.

"Commune"

"You are not alone in your suffering;
You are not the first to endure such things."

How abhorrent a species must we be
to find something of solace in shared pain.

Words spoken in placation-a ruse to spur a fainting life a little further,
a descending body to remain upright a little longer:
The placebo of hope
couched in the acknowledgement of universal torment.
And when the air itself is weight,
lights are fire, skin is exposed nerve
and the mind bludgeons itself,
we ask one to remain.

Perhaps we do not realize the substance of our words.

But it is understandable;
in those thickened and desperate hours,
we must find-or be given-some reason to inhale,
to accept that we do not yet wish to leave this world,
and string together such abject moments
grasped, or are mercilessly granted to us in our agony,
until that silent invocation is no longer true
and life becomes that which we fear...

"Weight"

What does the house feel, now, as the once-a-boy
walks upon its matted floors?
The weight of a familiar unfamiliar–
the same feet, though somehow altered,
the same hair, but coarser and less thick,
the same heart, now slower and less rhythmic.
Cuts from his childhood games resulted in unintended intimacy,
drops of saffron and of salt twisting into its wood or woven fibers,
others to be stemmed by a mother's hands,
washed into sinks with soothing words
accompanying their descent.
Sounds must pass with their initiators,
pre-pubescent sing-alongs to a flickering television moving into thumping
ballads,
and thence to withdrawn quiet, buzzing headphones driving thoughts away,
or deeper into a brain depressed or manic,
a brain of naïve certainties and mature doubts.
The arterial hallways, too, must have sensed what flowed along them,
parents chasing a glowing face at play, later chiding a glowering one that
hardened as it had stubbled,
still expressive in its way but more internally so, just as like to fume upon the
house
with fists and curses as it was to sear its own makers,
or burst itself behind closed doors.
But ringing, too, reverberates, as heated moments never won the hour,
and seats at the table were filled when life becalmed, or when appetites
overwhelmed the great complexities
and all sat to pacify their simple needs.
Comings home, the realignment of the ever-expanded universe of the
academic mind, gave reassurance, whether admitted to or not,
and evidential aging of both hosts and home were left unacknowledged.

Doors opened and closed, each time with greater interval, and life continued,
as much as ever it can,
until the three were left a pair, then less,
and the house hollowed.

Why has he now, that once-a-boy, chosen to cross again this threshold, when
time has calloused what was soft and silenced all the rest?
Do those rooms, those corners filled with sloughed skin and dust and memory,
those porous walkways and their heavy floors, welcome him?

It would tell us much to know, when the footsteps paused and the quiet began
to settle,
who was the first to speak.

"Autofill"

In every questioned moment it is there,
to answer queries random or direct;
Of urgency or boredom unaware–
indifferent to the choice that we select.
The presentation thought to be arranged
by counting of the souls that seek the site
And enter "Why," then "should," then "I," to change
or edify the thoughts that lurk at night.
What hungers met, what conscious streams erode
When partial ask placed upon a list;
Is back unburdened of oppressive load
through answer, or that "worse" in life exists?
Surprise is found that others wonder, too,
if this can be obtained, if such has worth,
how judgment stems from value misconstrued,
that one is not alone when on the earth.
An algorithm set to fill the blanks,
Responses unemotional or numb
May, unintendedly, deserve our thanks–
As questions show the will to not succumb.

"Trochees to Steinbeck"

One; to they who know a truth, is
All, and never doubting eyes proceed to
walk a causeway, sound, transgressions
cast to others–those of doubt–eschewed.

Open. Hated. Equal. Threatened. Pleasant. Brittle. Nourished. Smothered.

Flux. The waters turbid, silten,
thick; a flowing mixture, which, inspected,
teems with cores, foundations, given
temporary firmness when connected.

Allied. Scattered. Tethered. Distant. Mingled. Parted. Lucent. Murky.

Settling, patterns manifesting–
hazy if we see perspectiveless–if
eye and "I" are all; lost blessing
ever out of reach from lonely seraphs.

Knitted. Punctured. Melding. Rotted. Cognate. Shrouded. Growing. Final.

Two.

"Wear"

We open, and we close, ourselves to others–
And one wonders if, like a folded letter,
We begin to feel creased and worn in doing so.
Do those flexures in the cellulose reveal themselves
As canthal lines?

Perhaps the eyes are much more telling than we know.

"Rebound"

In ball, or thought, or echo hushed
reflection has a place–
As toy, idea, spoken word
is sent back towards the face;

But reconsideration may
Not have the chance to rise
As rubber, notion, statement blunt
Is thrust into our eyes.

While lack of caution in our games
a darkened bruise can bring,
Allowance of a wanton thought
can yield a baser sting.

But woe to one who speaks unchecked
of civics, likes, detests;
On mirrored screens in pockets, know
that judgment never rests.

"Harm"

Pain is sensed in gradients, and as
one man feverishly absorbs the scarlets and vermilions
of a morning birthed of July thunderheads
while another regards only something orange-red on the horizon,
so does it rise and ebb
from the conductivity of its flesh and liquid vessel.
       What unremembered gouge first brought the sensation to us–
       What purge of fluid–amniotic, milken– desperately convulsed
       set down affliction in the mind?
       Or light–the heavenly break of darkness–
       could light itself have seared through infant veils,
       making those eyes, those sea–blue windows
       not ready even to fathom the simplicity of the cradle,
       the apertures which welcomed that from which all life flees?
In all we do, in all our separate uniformity,
To this base edict do we bow, and in knowledge of
its inevitability
We shape a form resemblant–a selfish barricade
Of conscience golden, actions heroic, language soothing. Yet
all recede at end of day
to hide in corners as its walls are flayed.

To many, the sensation is met, endured;
Others, it overwhelms;
And to a desperate few, to numb a numbing,
The edict is reversed, and the harm embraced.

We each, in days not distant from the birth of light,
Discover which one of these we are.

"Words"

Oh, what possesses each of us
To talk of better days?
To sludge and limp with heads upturned
And wander over graves?

We tell ourselves that *it must end*
Before the true end comes;
For some, those words precede the choke
And in the grays succumb.

Our speaking out against the wind
Will never cease its blow;
No curses in the mirror stop
Minds losing what they know.

One shouts a sentence now to stem
The rushing stream of blood,
Which, flesh torn out by leaded steel
Incarnadines the mud.

Another coming in hushed tone
And lain on infant breast–
Imperatives and pronouns lost
In a consumpted chest.

A third exclaimed amidst hot tears
To pull a lover back;
They impotently ricochet
When hearts obscenely crack.

In every case, our artifice
Of diction falls away,
And, revealed then, the feebleness
In what we write and say.

How can our bodies, failing life
Live in printed word?
In ink and text beclouded, find
The thought of it absurd.

Forever futile, language seeks
Some everlasting home,
And we still cling to utterance--
Or write a transient poem.

II.

While an endless darkness and its punctuating fires surround our minute world,
we may absorb
the crackling of the grasshoppers in summer,
consider the somehow-directed rambling of the monarch,
and marvel at the unseen labor of a cloud before a birth of rain
to learn the wonder, and the peace,
of little things.

"The Storm"

Distant thunder warms the sky, while
sweeping waves, the air as misted
breath, transects the bowing wheatstems,
blows both rushing swallows and their
prey of glittering wing; they rise and
flatten–discombobulation–
sheets of wings and legs pursued by
feathered needles. In and out they
fly regardless, winds still chasing
in the constant push before the
silence, framed in mustard hues as
blended darkness grows. A cleft now
forms; an undulating shelf of
blue–black wool appearing while the
downdraft brushes treelines, sweeps the
ripe'ning fields–imagined as a
mane, instead, and rippling wither,
both responding in ecstatic
shakes to drops and winds descending.

Covert fissures, cloud–masked pulses
culminate in brilliant, jagged
ruptures, link again the earth and
sky–and one can almost feel a
current coursing down the twisted
wires, the posts affixed in sandy
soils compactless–soils abuzz to
ride the winds and join the shifting,
sliding hills' obscured advancement.
Sights and sounds in alternation
swim amongst the dusts, the flotsam

lifted out of ditch and culvert,
carved from blowout; air, too, varies
with direction, tempered only
when anticipation finds its
mate, and pauses tamp astriction.

Looming, stark, the fluid wall now
hastens; every sense engrossed in
rapt confusion, bodies choose to
fly, or run, to drift beside that
rolling Elemental, thriving,
pregnant with a yield befitting
lands of bosoms full, beatific.
Force, or forces, draws each form at
once to reverential bowing,
joining wheat and cedar, wings of
feathers and of glitt'ring crystal;
those of seeming evanescence,
momentary drops and pulses,
fissures, too, who walk upon the
prairie warm and waiting–who the
breezes gentle send from life, but
yet return in early summer,
rumbling, midst the clouds and dancing
grasses, exhalations thund'ring. . .

"Seed"

A simple, dangling pouch with fraying seams
Now still, no sensing pulses rapid, eyes
Awaiting sign instinctive, till they deem
The space from bough to thistle sack espied.

At last, a burst of crimson framed in browns
Electric in the flutter, dipping, just
A second, then alights upon the crown–
But slight achievement, surely, not to lust.

He bends to pluck a seed, once muscles loose
The delicate extraction–all is ease;
Another; three, when something felt obtuse
And, bolting, streaks the finch into the trees.

'Tis but a mundane movement through a pane
Yet one of percept few of us obtain.

"Separation"

I would have stopped, but I did not see-not until I couldn't stop.
It lay behind the mower, writhing, the brightest blood-blood is always so-
smearing onto the grass,
its head more than a foot away.

Was there a consciousness at all, some understanding of time dripping away?
Was there pain-or no pain at all? Taxes of the body severed, functions ending,
nothing for the mind to do but see and hear, taste saline on an arid tongue.
If it could have sensed, seen in my own head
That I never meant it harm,
that I felt a sorrow at my work,
would it have hated me regardless-
if hate is something such as they can feel.

I soon began again, and at some point finished,
and will, at some another point, do much the same,
our foolish urban husbandry.
Perhaps I will be more prudent, appreciative,
watch the butterflies a little longer,
or simply keep my lines
and think of disparate subjects.

"Early Harvest"

The lofty orchard ever obfuscated,
even on the widest, brightest days,
its trees bloom quickly, in flushing spring–summer,
their fruits ripening in their own peculiar pace
that Almanac or bone cannot predict;
and on day when air has thickened,
one's crop is ready, the produce transparent, glistening,
and without aid of picker, shaker,
trained or youthful hands
they fall, rolling in the blue–black and fitful winds,
agitating in their descent,
and like that sphere once plucked from Knowledge
each carries a kind of ruin to the earth . . .

"Flocking"

Identification through colors, refrains
To genus and species the subject adheres
No feature is aberrant, nothing abstained
Against the remarkable Nature does steer.

And so it would seem, as we look to the sky,
or up to the bough of an oak, towards a post;
Unique uniformity catches our eye
Its feathered sublimity leaves us engrossed.

Collectives distinct, individuals cloned
A forfeiture–maybe a need for conceit
For numbers conceal one–the group shields the lone
So, hidden in commonness, life can compete.

Is nothing, then, lost in the rounding of points
In flattened obscurement through endless recasts?
Regardless of brilliance–there's art in disjoints;
Survival of fittests the discrete outlasts.

In irregularity–still–is a strength
And deep in their history, ages ago,
Divergence appeared and, when tested at length
The standard was altered to that which we know.

So when, in observance of perching or flight
Beholding of pigments and chromatic sets–
A wafting of melodies sweet, bold, and right
Remember, we, Nature's apart from regret:

In each murmuration, in covies and stands
Else hiding in parliaments, cloaked in a skein
Lie idiosyncrasies, tests at Time's hands
Small peculiarities ventured for gain.

Know–Nature's an artist unrivaled in skill
And "abnormal" now may just govern our then
Don't see in a bird a form rigid and still–
Potential and wonder reside in the wren.

"Dimensions of the Air"

Textured, as with paint, the heavy oils of scent
collect upon the canvas of the day, even at this
early hour. The swallows move in a manner more of
ocean swimmers, on a current unseen but clearly palpable,
rocking in their facile navigation of the air. It is with effort that one moves,
and the hands unconsciously sweep before the face
as if to carve a pocket in the humidity to ease each breath.

One sense rises while another is confounded;
sounds enveloped, even to the point of suffocation, while
lilac and crab-apple blossoms lay wide at the stroke of even the most
gentle breeze.
The air is coated, seemingly, the shaking of leaves muffled
as the tongue, and mind, sweeten; one is immersed, and can imagine
trails of color mixing behind, curling,
for every life is artist, too, in the wanderings of spring.

The collection of pigments lies heavy upon the shoulders,
carried, almost as a mantle,
and equally as thick were one to run a hand over it,
yet it melts down the arms, the warmth
permeating skin and soul alike until all blends into a liquescent air,
at once weighty and
ethereal.

"Companions"

Dogs are great
Dogs are fun
Dogs are good for everyone.

Teeth bared, a ridge of fur centered along the spine, paws pressing
into the soil;
yet the boy smiles, knowingly,
as the picture is just for show. How far both have come,
we and the dog, that age-old
attendant who held its distance once, in fear or to plot its predatory approach,
but who has always circled the abodes of Man.

When, ages past, did one-starving and gaunt, lame from birth, simply curious-
first approach our fires? Or, perhaps, on some path,
it was we who stepped before-pups orphaned by fortune or flint
and, carried home, their innate wariness
receding through gifts of meat from tiny hands affectionate,
and sounds, before averse, of action and threats imminent,
coming softly from smaller mouths,
conveyed in somehow-universal expressions
of embracement.

Now, Man-and he not yet a man-rushes to those teeth, to those claws, both
animals expectant
to start the chase; and, whirling round, the dog
bursts out from well beyond the reach of what, forever ago, was desperate prey
or End incarnate, and runs with heated blood

and bounding exaltation away from joyous screams and pounding feet for but a
moment,
a simple moment, yet so much more–
the yield of twenty-thousand years.

"Secondary"

Up into the air, confidence climbing with the form itself,
they give that youthful frame its needed buoyancy,
while the fingered feathers–longer and searching–
grasp the sky.

Destined to shed by pulse of updraft, chance,
or shaken off at rest on distant perch,
–each having been gradually unfastened at Nature's wont through time–
theirs is a loss meant to be endured, and, as such, endurable.

The stiffened primaries, too, extensions of the body itself, will find the ground
as growth requires, to be rapidly replaced as easily as passing lust or thought;
but these first–fledged secondaries, swirling down
to slide into the blades of grass or drag along pavement into a refuse corner,
trembling,
have served their purpose,
brought that youth to flight–
and, having separated from their blood–tie,
will lift only through memory.

"Notice"

A person is never alone; there are always eyes upon you,
Ears above or below in anticipation or unease,
scents altering even distant forms of our approach,
tiny aviators steering clear, or alighting
for their purposes.
To some, Nature's omnipresence is unnoticed, while to others unwelcome,
even threatening.
A happy few see companions, guides, messages from a Creator,
blood-relatives, fellow pilgrims on a road of which they have a better view,
some greater understanding-a collective sentience through individuals with
colors
beyond our skill to reproduce, abilities no mythic hero possesses, sizes
miniscule and massive, and focus-or passivity-that we simply cannot mimic.
Microcosms of the world itself, and all harmonious and beautiful.

Until the bite.

"Drift"

The scent thrills, even before perception,
before its name alights in the mind and the back straightens,
the spine tenses. It is to us as our tang is to the wilder ones,
and all the senses join to warn of danger.
And so rekindled is a biological imperative, for most long-smothered,
yet for those who have islanded in seas of grass,
in foothills matted with brush or matchstick pine
it lays warmer.

From whence, how far, and of what–
from bin or firepit, flames licking slats upon a charcoal grill–nothing more,
or something unconfined and eager.
"Could be from anywhere–got a good breeze going today" one says,
the true implication of the words coming after.
In such a manner is that acrid wisp turned over in the brain while the body
readies–the bones and muscles wiser, tempered–
and eyes scan the horizons for a sign before,
as we are wont to do, insulating ourselves from notions of harm
through a clever recitation of converging circumstances,
primitiveness of foreign lands and the improvidence of strangers,
excuses to belie the possibility.

Removed in time and circumstance from that once–bulwark
against the Darkness, our primal and primary foe,
we have forgotten how our age'd evening consort was ever a fickle one,
and frolics where it pleases.

"Personification"

So the bark of the tree is skin, aged, sun-spotted in the resiliency of
maturation,
and the tree itself reaches upward as if to grasp the light.
The trunk of the tree is its body, warped with time
and efforts made to shift or lean,
and showing scars of procedures and examinations, even amputations,
but still sound,
still full of life.
Roots-the feet and legs-are mostly hidden, though they move in their way
though deep recesses in the soil,
and some are exposed, the winds and time-again-revealing what was tender
in the swaddling earth and now is scaled and knobby, yet holding firm below.
The tree-our verdant self, our figurative doppelganger-stands ready,
ready to be the representation of our feelings, haunting the edges of
Halloween, bowing reverentially on April mornings; even naked, deep in
winter, reminding us of potentials and resurrections.
It is always of our seasons-as we so choose, we who translate the world.

But what else of us, then, do we accord?
Are we to burden the tree with suffering, too-
Letting it ache when curious children peel away that bark, or
those on the border of adulthood carve into its quick
a pair of names, destined to last far longer than their lust, even their love-
and darker seasons that follow naive thoughts
of happy boughs waving in the spring?
Will it be forced to scream in vain as its children are spread to die,
as ever upward and away it grows from those that,
against the calculus of time and chance, survive?
Shall doubt and desperation rot it from within, too, until
the masque of bark and flesh are all that remains of a hollowed life,

while questioning the significance of anything
as it, and us, are wrenched from out the earth?

How charitable we are
To refrain from giving all.

"Zeniths"

The dawn reveals only the flame itself,
for cascading warmth is unceasing once the year has passed it midway point,
the Solstice serving as the harbinger of the coming heat-and
no ebony blanket, Sirius-etched, can smother it.

These dog-days, from which their less-celestial namesakes hide in the scant
shadows—
of houses, cars, even mailboxes, until their owners,
seeing their plight, free them back into their societal and air-conditioned
confinement,
and they eagerly scamper in, heads bowed, tongues lolling.

All is extended, stretched; the trees are at their height,
and the invisible cicada, whose voices disappear at our approach,
seek ever higher reaches as they emerge, having crawled
from the placental soils
into this realm of giants. Ascending, with movement clumsy and yet sure-
how many inches, how many feet until their transformation, only they know-
and ripping through their larval skin into a beady drop of luminescent white-
green,
they gaze upward, waiting for their wings to fill with fluids stored for that very
purpose
inside that brown and land-tied shell.
Now, their metallic vibrato rings through the trees
and drips down to echo off of sidewalks, themselves seeming to hum
from the torridity.

Deep in summer, we are all aboriginal, running with steaming skins to the
waters and back again—and we, unstated, hope
an alike purification follows, or a reinvigoration through the channeling of
youth,

youth that speeds its sleep along to bring another day of ponds or pools,
of possibility,
hearts feverous as sun-baked brows.

The sun seems to bear down upon us, demands us keep our distance-
or rather the earth is holding us more dear, as if we were soon to desiccate and
be spiraled upwards in the dust-devils, those whirls of heat,
our energy transmuted to a rising gyre, away from us-
vitality sapped with thoughts of bodies moving off,
glances unreturned.
It is then the halls of schools begin to beckon,
distant spots of rest receding in the rearview mirror
and sun rolls downhill now, its angle dropping daily, almost,
shadows lengthening;
and heat, its hold slipping,
hollows the voice of the cicada
perhaps in some last attempt to call
those skins and hearts back to its embrace.

III.

I do not believe that Death lies in wait;
perhaps it simply wanders, like the rest of us,
searching for a place where it is needed.

"Gone"

Time seems endless, unknowable,

and we live for the smallest fraction of that time, miniscule drops in the stream;

but there was a last moment, a singular, distinct point, before we existed–

the world without us,

one that we didn't know, couldn't know,

held no sway, altered no courses. Unimaginable to us–a place

of no consciousness.

Then, we were, we arrived, we "became"; our own Big Bang.

None of us knew what could, would, nor hoped *should*–follow. Think:

try to remember every detail, every second that we have spent on this world as

it floats in the darkness, each of us living on our own unchartable timeline,

then understand that nothing, and no one, exists on its own:

We have engraved upon individuals in intimacy and in passing,

left names on documents,

written lines in digital letters on a digital expanse and sent them on their way,

walked on shorelines and on concrete,

placed our heels upon the dust,

eaten and slept and vomited and coughed–

cried, prayed, laughed, felt the waves from oceans and,

if we were most fortunate,

far stronger waves in the heart from the love of another.

In the end, we lose that world, and if we are given the opportunity

for a final time, will think of what that first blank moment–now,

after us–will be.

Unimaginable.

Yet the world will have noted us, in some small way,

to its betterment or its disappointment,

seen us for our granted time, felt our footsteps,
collected our tears, absorbed our
hate, our laughter, our word–garbage and wasted energy,
seen us desperate or content, watched us think upon a sunset,
grasp at memories fresh or fading,
received our parents, our friends,
our broken bodies, and–
perhaps a soul escapes
–all that we are. All.

But we were here, and the world knew us–
and that, I think, is something.

"Laying of Hands"

"He's gone."

      One-Two-Three-Four.

"Man, there's nothing. He's out. Got no pulse."

      One-Two-Three-Four. Keep it up.

      One-Two-Three-Four.

"Please! Help him!"

      One-Two-Three-Four.

"Would've bled out by now anyway. Look at that."

      One-Two-Three-Four.

      One-Two-Three-Four.

"Ma'am, I'm sorry."

      One-Two-Three-Four. Keep it up. C'mon.

      One-Two-Three-Four.

"Get away from me! Please, help him. Please!"

      One-Two-Three-Four.

"Sir, I've got to get him covered. Too many people."

      One-Two-Three-Four.

"God damn it! I'm sorry! God…damn it, damn it…"

      One-Two-Three-Four. Keep it up.

      One-Two-Three-Four.

"Sir, you've got to move now. Got to move."

      One-Two-Three-Four.

      One-Two-Three-Four. Yeah, I know.

"Never felt nothing. Look at the car."

      One-Two-Three-Four.

"We've got a job to do. Gotta let us in."

      One-Two-Three-Four. Stay with it.

      One-Two-Three-Four.

"No! Get away-please! No!"

      One-Two-Three-Four.

"Sir. Hey."

One-Two-Three-Four.

One. Two.

One.

"Ok. Just–ok. Ok."

One-Two-Three-Four.

"Fifteen"

Life is an engraving of tiles, a number placed by simple order of encounter
upon the brilliant ivory squares of our memories;
Firsts of many kinds may show their faces there–a quickening heart electrified
by two earth-brown orbs of oblivion; an undoing of a trust; the discovery or
deprivation of a furred companion, a friend forever–
but our minds, though seemingly limitless, imposes an
order of operations on the board, and soon we realize
that the most ebony stained,
most deeply etched of terrors and revulsions
push those more sublime and sweetened recollections to the margins,
then off the edge.
Our task becomes increasingly desperate as we try to move those darkened
numbers away and re-establish order, with our chosen memories–
those of love, of solace and companions, of vistas wide–

those that should have made us something vivid,
made us Something–

finding the hallowed spaces.

But always are we fighting the accumulation of the awful, images bloated and
searing and desperate,
and these gravitate northwest, for us to repeatedly displace.
We find success at first, as every shift not only pushes these in distance
but envelops them for a time with brighter visions. Yet
soon we notice patterns, soon we see that the sequences find limits,
the arrangement becoming ever less alterable,
and observe, too, that the etchings have begun to bleed,
tainting those they neighbor,
and movement smears and spreads even when the numbers recede again
through force.

In anguish, we persist–but more and more we are outmaneuvered by simple chance

and errors committed in our blurred distress

until those infant firsts are overwhelmed, mobbed by the punishing wreak of time and misconstruction,

then relegated to that most distant corner of our consciousness as the board fills with shadow.

At such a point, even the nimblest of fingers,

illustrated outwardly as they press upon a scarred temple

cannot reorder quick enough,

fail to recall either the momentary harms of youth or those perfumed memories,

and begin to doubt any supposed objective

in taking up the game.

"Evening"

Nighttime wind, a blanket of sound
      Laying upon packed–stretched shoulders,
      a back perspiring–
      draped over one too tired to
      don a drier shirt, who
      gladly takes the sweat–soaked garment
      as a pillow, and one content
            To lend the stars his labor
            and the earth his weight

Nighttime wind, a curtain of sound
      Laid upon pack–broken shoulders.
      a trunk perspiring–
      shrouding one too weary to proceed
      in the gathering darkness
      one who contentedly takes the buffalo grass
      for a pillow, eager
            To give to the stars his labor
            And to the earth
            His weight

"Disunion"

The mind is malleable, fluid, of a sheen at once brilliant and serene;
but in its foundation,
there is something else–
a fault, perhaps, opaque through its quicksilver–
something that tilts its pooled balance and
unlevels all, makes it move
to this direction or to that.
More than the simple ripple that comes from
an unknown scent, an event surprising,
a random date, encountered in a textbook,
or any simple drop of information which,
dissolved, becomes part of the understanding.
It is not uncommon for such a drop to result in
momentary confusion as the swimming particles
consider what it is, where in that great mirrored pool
of teeming information
it may best integrate inside the basin of our skull.
No.
There comes a shaking, a shift,
and the precious liquid rushes to one side, in crashing waves
that fold upon themselves,
and all that we have seen and felt, our loves
and dreams, our hates, beliefs,
our certainties and doubts and plans and memories of things unsaid, undone
begin to separate and find themselves alone, no longer homogenous
or at the very least diluted to a lesser potency–
and they leap up, exposed, then plunge, again and again,
with any areas of coalescence slamming into each other, violent and
thundering,
tempestuous ringings and alarumns;
the body jerks and rages, screams out in desperation,

an individual drowning in the mind,
grasping out at anything to find correction, calm.
And while external interventioning may later give those waves a
more distant shoreline,
time to disperse, or counterbalance,
for now it, too, is slave to the momentum that,
if blocked, will send the surge against the other side
and
set the whole aboil, a churning vomitus.

At such times do all things fail, and one wonders if Time
which, through its workings of patient exhaustion, cools all that we are
can ever order, ever pair those drops and particles again
or if, years from the rocking and the quaking,
and ostensibly beyond the last of its transmitted riffles,
we are even recognizable.

"Balloon"

A child with a balloon. A trope, a cliché,
sketched by almost every artist as some point or another.
Yet there he was and that little once-flat slip of filled latex, nothing else-and
his expression showed no want for more.
Bouncing along the ground, batted in the air, rubbed against the hair
and then sticking to the wall, defying gravity.
A dozen for $1.25, and the air always in supply,
especially in the breaths of youth.

Is it the shape that so engages him? This little airy sphere,
dancing along unseen the curvature of that oh-so-consequential one
on which we live and die,
the circularity of Nature itself,
its roundness, eternally pregnant with possibility;

Or consider the breaking of lines, of material barriers,
a solid becoming "other" in growth before our eyes,
colored air-drops inside our unforgiving walls and echoing corners;

Perhaps it is the animation, for to a limp form life is given,
and now it moves,
responds, adheres or jumps away almost in sentience,
moves along a course of its own choosing, seemingly,
though dictated by unseen currents and charges of which the child is ignorant
and finds itself at last at peace in soft and youthful hands,
towering adults seemingly powerless to grasp it, grasp its purpose even,
their impotence of understanding inexplicable to childish eyes.

It must be these.

But maybe it's just fun.

"Movement"

Accumulating lives upon the grille
These instantly becoming grains of loss
Displayed for those that join along the miles
As, rushing, travelers navigate across

the country. No one seeks the massacre,
and while we may regret the small events
it neither brings a comment for the wind
or reconsideration of intents.

An act is termination, also growth–
if not for us ourselves of those in kind–
and life is movement, ever must be so,
acknowledging our bodies are consigned.

To stay in place is withering, if one
is meant to run; considering the ends
and counting damages will not retard
the slaughters, nor the darker facts suspend.

We have to seek, to go, to ambulate
for others on the road we then will meet
and in collective life is strength and pulse–
–and more–that make an apart soul complete.

And so it is with Nature where the one,
behind, remains, for benefit of they;
We ache, and should, for any life, resigned
Yet onward must we go to make our way.

"Rot"

"What? Oh-that. It's nothing."

"I don't know-just noticed it one day. Had it a while now."

"No, doesn't hurt, sometimes just itches."

"Pretty much the same. Maybe a little bigger. Don't think about it much."

"Come on-stop hassling me. A little discolored, I guess. Skin's still mostly white."

"Why worry about it? We don't have that stuff in the family."

"I don't care what everyone else says."

"Maybe I'll get it looked at. That make you happy? I'd know if there's a problem."

"Whatever. It'll take care of itself."

"Refuse"

"A person should not focus on the material. Remember: you cannot take it with you."

But what do we do
when the only things left are only things? Chairs,
trinkets, glossy photographs, cellular phones,
favorite sweaters, shoes worn and those worn only once,
blush and watches and mascara and dishes and pens and mirrors–
some meaningless and some too meaningful.
How can we throw away, give away anything that they have touched, when
they will touch nothing else now, including us?

It is true that you can't take it with you–
but they took everything else with them. So, so much.
Everything outside of memories bouncing in a strained and darkened mind,
memories that you cannot put on a shelf, cannot clutch, that often
make it all hurt more.
Why can't we just skim and let the rest sink away?

If any "thing" has value, it's because of us. So now we stare at piles of summer
clothes and heavy coats, alarm clocks, kitchen clatter, rakes and shovels, balls of
twine and wire saved for needs that never came,
pants and socks and fingernail clippers, spice jars and half-boxes of tissues and
delicates not meant for us to see and the pictures we drew as stupid kids not
worth the saving tucked nearby. A little money in an envelope. Gum. Car
keys and purses and wallets. Cards of plastic proving they exist. That they
existed.

No, they wouldn't have wanted to burden us. No, they do not think that any
of it really matters now. It's ok. They wouldn't have wanted us to stand
there, trying to find

the place between all and nothing.

But there has to be a something for the hands, the eyes, a scent still fresh
enough, the familiar. Something. That's what's here now,
so, so much of it.

No, they wouldn't want to burden us.

But they have to understand that we need it, that
memories are just too soft to bear the weight alone.

"Doubt"

Maybe theirs is a better way.

Instinctual, the following of cellular directions
as if written in a ledger, to be passed along
without wonderment.
A birth, and feedings at the teats dispassionate,
with only hunger and the basic pulls of physiology
connecting her and this little one.

Following behind, doing only as has been seen,
some keep up, some disappear,
and brief is the response.

Then, a day–no stars on a calendar,
no rites of passage presaging much to come and much left behind,
that young one wanders away, turns the other direction,
stops following. No trepidation, no tears from she or it,
and evidence of any loss, if somewhere deep in neural caverns,
is missing. "They" is pulled apart by Nature, but nothing
indicates resistance.

And then no pages full of pictures turn in hands of thinning skin;
no staring at a silent phone,
And lovies held in trunks amidst the smallest clothes
do not fill darkened rooms or recesses
or enter into thought.
And even other broods replace what once had suckled, once had stepped
or jumped in playfights
behind its mother,
new lives following along without a care, or fear, or any cognizance
of future changes, losses, paths alone.

As simple as the blinking of an eye, or a breath exhaled
seems life outside humanity,
and so perhaps it is. But we seem not of such a world,
and the soft cheek of a son or daughter
remains more dear, more potent
than all the pain and desperation it may afford
regardless.

"Beal Slough"
(In Memory of Marilyn McArthur, Professor of Nursing / Dedicated to Al DiMauro, Professor of English and Humanities)

Perhaps it had been enough of a life.

Many faces, young faces, must still have been inside, somewhere; each in a beginning, wading tentatively, on journeys towards healing others. Dedicated faces, soon to serve, for none is an island.

And colleagues-as you, aging-amidst the endless flow of youth, the flow you ushered for just a little while to an estuary filled with mortar boards.

Alterations seen in them, in their lives, and in your own. Such a life of ebbs and rushing waters.

Perhaps that is what drew you there, the movement, the purposefulness of the slough. To find those faces once again, to see them in the stream of time when life was clear, not turbid; when you did not have to endure the disappearances, the theft of mind.
It's so difficult to remember now.

What dam had broken, finally, after decades eight; what pull of sorrow overwhelmed, darker waves eroding that contented margin and gentle shoreline—memories of your life now dissolving, breaking apart, moving into some unsounded elsewhere?

Family. Confusion. Friends. Hollowness. Remembrance of bodies healed, spirits healed. Uncertainty and desperation.
I just can't remember.
Was it finally too much?

Perhaps you went to stare into the holy, the baptismal, seeking blessing for a life now lost. Perhaps to wash it away.

You are buoyant now, in the calm waters. There is the certainty.

And we will remember for you.

"Away"

The fall of a mind does not happen as a storm,
as pulsing incandescence or shattering winds.
It's not like the movies.
You just lean away from what is of concern, of rational import, and
begin to wander, with the sound of conversation and the focus of the eyes
dimming.
It is so easy, so passive, and the jaunt sometimes pleasant.
Then you return to an expected glance as the question wasn't answered,
maybe a confused look,
and at first it is brushed off, everyone's normal resumes.
But they don't know how much you are gone when alone, when no one is
there
to see the fluttering, the fueling highs and impenetrability, nor
the submerging, the drowning of the spirit at your nadir
and the attempts at escape that follow.
And so it goes, but the distance on those ramblings stretches,
they come more often, and some people go away,
or their expressions stay strange–
and sometimes what was felt and seen
in those imagined vignettes comes back with you,
and maybe so does a resistance–
the other place having been severed but you're what's bleeding,
or it's like you've just come from the womb
but do not have the virgin ignorance of the child who only cries at cold and
brightness, not
those darker things.

And on an ordinary day
–shaving, at the desk and chair like every Tuesday, on a run, scrolling, washing
it all down at a bar–
you simply keep walking, everyone's normal stays behind, and they stay, too.

And perhaps you're lucky enough that one there to witness in a helpless way,
or to say that everything will be ok,
and who knows; maybe you get pulled back, now exposed for what you are
yet having hope and a hand to tether you,
but maybe it's already kind of ok in that other place–
or there is only bewilderment or terror
and
nothing

"Spectres"

Can there be such as happy memories
When immaterial they are?
Of families, friends, and firsts they rise in mind
But at a distance ever far.

So very little in our lives is clean–
Without the stain of error, mar;
Adulterated now by loss and time
These purest people, times are scarred.

We reach for them when life finds us in need
and they appear without regard
to what effect their narrowness will have,
what seal will now be left ajar.

How can a recollection, quiet and thin,
Held in that soundless reservoir,
Flood with such joy that sweeps away what is
And leaves reality bizarre?

Then, left with knowing the remembered is
As lines retold in a memoir,
Descriptive, true, but flattened to the page,
Their animation, souls disbarred.

Without them, we are lost, yet lost with, too,
For real has gone from what they are;
Impalpable, obscure these spectral views–
Yet still as bright as any star.

"Sight"

I saw it, then
it saw me-or I imagined it as so.
A glittering, from paces away, and footsteps all around;
the flashing stayed, and left, and came again.
It lay, by some innate avoidance or just a trick of chance, unbroken,
though not whole-for neither frame nor mirrored twin remained nearby.
A lens-a
simple shard of glass,
poured or molded, curved, ground, and set; sent from an
unknown somewhere to a somewhere else with countless
others, in frames eclectic, simple, black and of every shade but black-
boxes of sight, or vision, of a thing unhad.

Just there, upon a sidewalk, it looked up-and through it came the sunlight,
An eye of pure white, almost, its proper eye long gone. The odds
of its survival, outpaced by the odds of its return, swam through my head,
as did the thoughts of what it had beheld, with who, and for how long.
What did its invention allow that nameless one to seen? Had smiles of
children, or their screams of separation, bounced upon its surface? Were
friends or lovers countenanced?
Tears-of joy? Of endings?-pooling at its edge against the cheek,
or screens, flickering, lines of code,
emails, letters noting balances unpaid,
stories bound in cloth of a world long ago, or fantasies of those to come-
the wafting ghosts of lattes, the splattered droplets from cans of beer opened in
revelry, in pain-
of comings and goings and waiting and hoping and living and dying,
and resting, finally, upon a nightstand,
exhausted,
with no views left before it.

The passers-by wondered at me, no doubt, as I hovered over
what they did not observe, or cared not to,
and reaching down, I touched it once to feel its cleanness,
its clarity;
then, thinking back,
I raised my heel
and crushed it into nothing.

IV.

If you cannot be someone's flame,
Be that someone's light.

"All"

How many pictographs in sooted caves,
or figures incised on clay, carved in stone–
how many lines have risen from the heart
onto papyri, vellum, precious cloth,
incarnadined and inked, with words of love?
The cloistered quill, the pen, the pencil, etch
on block of stone or wood or heavy lead,
to letterpress or pounded type in rooms
aclatter, next then strung with colored wires
to transmit screen to sheet until the word
on bands and channels surfs, and cellulose
transmutes to scrolls of code inside a cloud.

Such evolution is of little note.
Though time ensures our tools are not the same,
deficient still the words in every quote;
ineffability of love's to blame.
So digital replaces stone–and, near,
a screen's conductive oxide ochre ousts;
and while with signals science interferes,
same analogues for love writers espouse.

For it is liquid warmth infused by kiss;
the smile of eyes on linens bright with sun;
upon the tongue arancia's glistening drops;
a night of wheeling stars and beckoning dreams;
perfumed and slickened skin in passion's brace;
that song which holds sweet memories intact;
our laughs, in youth, discovering the rain;
to learn a whispered voice can charge the heart;

the lightness of the End with family near;
it is the water's cleansing, lifting hands;
invincibility at every breath.

The only, All, in fields of gold at play
And ever that beyond our words to say.

"Return"

It was the quiet that caught my attention,
pulled me up from checking my own receipt.
Charger. Wrong cable.

Words spoken clearly, not in whisper-then, silence. A perverse silence-
one that communicated the strangeness, or the severity, of the act,
the incredulity of those who witnessed. Just me, and her. And him.

His words preceded a slow friction, friction of something being pushed
forward,
pushed away.

"You-you want to return this?"

"Yes."

"You mean exchange? Ok. There's lots of others, and cheaper. Just leave it
here, and you can go choose-"

"No."

I shouldn't eavesdrop.

"Just return. I don't need it. I have my receipt."

Quiet again. Then keys pressed, register drawer opened, bills pulled with few
coins. She counted them for him, delicately.

"Thank you."

He turned, she, too-quickly averting her eyes to the receipt that hadn't been checked, or her nails,
or maybe again at blue card with the wisp of pink flowers,
its black script of swirling cursive too small to read from where I was.

He walked away-more like fell away. Heavy, all of it. Must have felt it, too, as he straightened up, adjusted-maybe prepared himself for leaving.
For whatever lay outside.

I shifted my weight, started to raise my foot. *Insensitive. Ridiculous. Patronizing.* Tried to run through the reasons. *What to say about it, anyway?* I didn't even know what "it" was.

"Sir"?

Right.

"Sorry," I spoke with half-attention, watching. Through the scanners. Out the exit. Gone.

"I need to return-exchange this" setting the charger and receipt down on the now-crowded surface.

You don't need to look. You should not look.

"Ok," she said, almost staring at me. Maybe I was the one staring, trying to harness something.

Silence.

And we didn't move.

"Diameter"

A lonely one is preferable to an unhappy two,
even if they are only marginally so.
We all spiral in life, whether upwards or down, and often
simply at level, content in our sight-line or too timid to gauge other views.
And loneliness intensifies, in an outwardly quiet and inwardly desperate whirl,
That centripetal force becoming too ponderous to maintain, and it is then
pushed out-and soon,
like a pinball, and similarly ever angling downwards,
the spinning and the ricochets are uncontrollable.

But it is only so wide; those hoping hands that
once-if once-held fast
to each other, at least to the idea,
create a greater range, and the imbalance of unhappiness
-for the two feel it, and bear it, differently, though it is their shared creation-
brings flailing, grotesque and desperate,
as if one tries to throw the other off to stop the spin but only makes it worse,
so the two are wild in their throes of suffering,
and their unavoidable dismemberment, if any must bear the seeing it,
is far-reaching and horrific.

Yes.

Such peculiar thoughts appear from time to time in the mind of those alone.
How strange for they who would give up the world for another,
and in who the general force of nothingness seems
quite enough.

"Love Story"

"Do you . . . ?"

"I do."

"Will you both . . . ?"

"We will."

"Why can't you . . . ?"

"I thought I was."

"Why don't we . . .?"

"I thought we were."

"Are you . . . ?"

"I am."

"Can't we . . . ?"

"Ascent"

Three feet upon the creaking stair
his hesitancy grows;
Both houses lean-just one aware
the ticking pulse now slows.

And with the weakness gaining strength
he claws the skin-worn rail
ascending, here, the given length
of lit and darkened trail.

Now following familiar slats
and tracing mind and step
the fire-path fifty years had fanned
to window where it leapt.

With slight reluctance, the lone man
before the boarded sill
stands both to feel where it began
where, now, they cease their will.

For when she gave the pane her weight
that which the body held
and let light take her, mind prostrate,
His frame and soul were felled.

And so, he, searching for the space
Where casing, plank meet not,
He pulls, the strain bright in his face,
To take the path she wrought.

"Incomparable"

Intelligence is rare;
Intelligence mantled with beauty even more so;
And when humanity is the bond of these,
No blushed diamond nor alpine desert bloom
Is as exquisite.

"Concepire"

Minds are most capable; zeniths, nadirs conjure
Ecstasy, Hopelessness, each in its turn. In our
endless potential we craft joys and fears, and the
Labor's production is profit, concern; but one's
Who is superior–thus, now transume and do
linger on beauty, absorbing its light, and like
wandering swallows seek warmth, to commune beyond
sharpening winds, set exquisite in sight.

Who cannot claim to have found himself hypnotized
even at thoughts of the scent of another, of
secreted touches, cascading desires, slips of the
glinting of sunlight on brown locks that smother, hair
which, over star-painted shoulders cascades with those
passions, the eye tracing curves, then converging at
last on a face intercessional; staid is that
word, for reality separates, swerves from the
mind, and no focus remains, long or quick, but a
urge to embrace, or to drown in her eye-pools, where
no trepidation is found; or to liquify
onto her lips as they quiver in repliant
Harmony–for, if concordantly, she discerns
Scents, traces profiles, is drawn to his lashes, his
Jawline, his mouth in accompaniment, see, then, all
Else fall away; and a "they," thus impassioned, now
know that all doubting has ceased. Then envelopment follows, in twining of
limbs, keen caresses, or
simply enclosing their hands; and the swell mimes the
pulse of their coupling hearts' inflamed essences.

This, then, is hope, it is wonder, enchantment; the

unified two now a new world can chart. As a
Whole, such is dear, such is blessing-instill in the
soul that the joining of two is life's art; and know
instantiation exists for you all and your
Vision-*bellezza perfetta*-divine; purpose
manifest, whether the truth of such call may be
found in that corporal One---or the mind.

"Babble"

Travelers, we seek the keys to the continents, their peoples,
terra lingua words and phrases of casual construction–
"*¿Ďonde está el hotel, señor?*"
when lost,
"*Quanto é este?*" to a street vendor,
or even a simple "*Piacere.*"

Learn and articulate, deliver just so; words deployed to open doors,
such tricks of tongues.

How much more is said by us ourselves, as flesh, in static silent frame,
especially in those moments that carve themselves into the bones;
how lingual is a simple smile,
guarding or quizzical the brows,
mere frames to those so-telling eyes that plead, repel, laugh in themselves,
explore–
or lust, when, fearful that words will say too much, we demur in opening
the mouth, yet lay all bare without intention;
the hands, too, shoved in pockets as if to hide a vulnerability,
at other times sails to speed along our sound,
pointed threats in fingers numbed,
or spread apart in exaltation as the loved appear before them.
Even the hair itself communicates,
whether wind enliven it or it reposes,
maybe twined upon the shoulders,
or brushed aside in annoyance, embarrassment,
the hands giving a different interpretation of the mover's act
as sweat-beads form on he who watches coffee locks re-set behind the ears.

Oh, how inconsequential do seem words
even from smiths and orators adept
when all it takes is scented skin of tan
and contracted eye
for one to bow before the Deliverer.

"Innamorare"

We fight so many battles, die and live through wars of a thousand kinds
inside and out, encounter doubt and uncertainty-
but when we think of "Love," we have no trepidation, see no conflict,
need no edification:
It is beautiful, weightless yet gravitational, wonderous-and it is either present,
or it is not.

Attempt to describe it, and you'll fail; try to explain it, and you'll fall short. It
is the same for everyone. That does not seem to vex us, though,
for it can simply *be* "indescribable" or "inexplicable",
unlike anything else on this earth,
Love needs no analysis,
no definition, no categorization--and it is never opposed. Even its
disappearance is embraced-"better to have loved and lost" and all that.
It is THE universal positive, yet unknown, unpredictable, and uncontrollable.
Uncontrollable.

Try not to love;
we rise each morning knowing what is and is not, what should and
shouldn't be:
this is right, this wrong; this is too expensive, this affordable; this adheres to
law, this does not; there is time, or there is none; and even the anomalous
comes down to a "Yes" or a No" when something "feels right" or doesn't.
It's all binary, mechanical, simple.
Then, it happens. It's here.
Try not to love;
try to explain why it shouldn't be, cannot be, what edict it violates, how
dangerous is the idea-and you, again, will fail. Try to restrain it, smother it,
cut it away, press into in a recess, and it lives on, a life-force unencumbered
by the weight of the physical, free to go where it chooses, into whom, and, in
its purest form, between whom.

Try not to love;
look at it, evaluate, consider all the variables, Not immoral. Not a matter of means. No broken law. All there is, is time. And of course it feels "right." It, then, must be "good." How could it possibly be otherwise? The universal positive. Always.

Maybe. Maybe that indescribable and inexplicable, though, is just sometimes, somehow, wrong after all.

But you go ahead. Try not to love. Just try.

We'll fail.

V.

We must each set our lives to a bearing,
and whether we lose our way or fall along the path,
never reaching our endpoint,
that simple act of orientation will sustain.

"Maps"

We all have our maps, our plotted course to an imagined destination–
crafted in the mind with both careful consideration of the panorama
that life has so far shown us
and an epistemological innocence–
that the world must simply be extension of what we know,
that we will remain safe as we have been.
So are all explorers children, staring from the doorstep on an afternoon in
spring.

But we know nothing of the elevation changes,
peaks and valleys or forests strewn with deadfall,
the waters which must be crossed,
the peoples, brute or benevolent and neither so different, upon whose lands
–if ever the earth in in our purview–
we may find ourselves as strangers,
the endless oceans, even
the continents that lay before us.
All is imagined, and every step finds alteration.

What drives us forward, having found our concepts fragmented or false,
our invincibility defeated, and
boundaries insurmountable–
the naïve conviction of that first step long lost,
and in our dawn now stupefaction,
the reeling mind loosed to a vision that,
on one spring day, was not even conceivable?
And what becomes of our first paper worlds,
before we find the guidance of the heart or the pull of coin and custom,
smears of paint or greasy crayon on heavy colored scraps,
one perhaps enough, for all its faults and foolishness,
to be magneted to an icebox?

The earth is layered with our mistaken maps,
errors of striplings and sages,
and most are lost while some, in peculiar fashion, are deemed of note.
And yet we continue to draw,
in our ignorance and in our hope,
and somehow lay upon them the foundations
of great cities, parks of trees and swings,
libraries, stores of now-necessities, halls of learning,
and homes of youthful certainty,
their doorways broad.

"Genesis"

So. There must be moment, private inspection
Before any movement to map a reflection

Of a part, or the whole, of what floats on the sphere
Perhaps just past one's croft, or far distant from there.

In the act must be purpose, but does that last come
From the edict of monarch, the bob of a plum

Dropped in a bowl of clear water, the sight bringing
Thoughts of our place on this earth, of beginnings and

Edges; in a desperate drive to comprehend
Where our feet have transected, where lands have an end.

In a due course, then, the preparations commence,
Knowing all must adhere to the chosen intents;

In quarters surrounded by crosses and chanting,
By curved or peaked window, the eastern light slanting;

Perhaps Pacific mists caress light silken screens–
While the vantage may differ, and so may the means,

The creator, in cloak made of overwrought wool,
Or a tunic of gold or of saffron, is full

With a Vision, a story to match with his world,
And through delicate hands these unite and unfurl.

This old-world cartographer's worn easel sits low
And, his stool checked for balance, he shifts for best glow,

Scrutinizing the workspace, lamp, compass, and charts
The latter for guidance, but oft bent in the art;

And, then, application-onto vellum quite thin-
A sable streak of ink on the acceptant skin

Into delineations of province and realm,
Navigating the borders of knowledge; at helm

He commands us, while, ever attempting to show
That which is correct and unquestioned—what we know,

Proceeding past the limits of mind, to impart
A belief-a construction beyond sight, in heart.

The quill in mimesis, turning round into flat
And the dark boundaries glisten, recreating that

Which may never appear on the ground, parse the glade-
From the intrigues of state, phantom borders are made.

With the form of the countries, domains now complete
He will ponder if records, abstraction can meet

To make this map unique, depict more than the rest
And this can be achieved through what none can attest

As while errors in names and missteps will occur,
"Embellishment" may stretch past what he can concur;

For a contest exists, and while "right" has rewards
It is often the first, most-marveled that accords

The high praise and the coin, both ill-fitted for this
Pursuit of coordinates, of pathways through mists

That retain, that restrain us from looking abroad
For maps form the route between confirmed and untrod.

Yield to temptation and speculation wins out,
the map will be marred and become shaded with doubt,

but-peculiar-in a different time, that map may
be a collector's piece for its aberrant way.

In the now, the pen must remain servant to real;
The artist, withal, stays cognizant of appeal,

So after the places and rivers are plotted,
Valleys and mountains, later hachured, are dotted

Or drawn as mere hills, crafted small due to the scale-
That conversion dictating the detail, a fail

In the choice, and the map may just augment a wall,
Ostentation is beautiful, useless withal.

Application-the document's ultimate use
Must determine the medium, scale-else obtuse

It will be to the landowner, emigrant, friar
Who, journey found impractical, gives it to fire.

Thus, for every map extant, one-hundred are gone
Torn, stained, mangled, rotted, blindly jotted upon;

Insect-eaten, child=trampled, coated with grime,
Or lost in the detritus through passage of Time;

For one-hundred reasons-and the greatest must be
That obsolete it became when more we could see.

In the moment, our skilled, patient map-maker inks
His lines, waters, town names, even peoples, and thinks

Of the margins ,wide oceans, lacunae, bare wastes
And he contemplates how to address that white space

If colors are feasible-ground ores, pressed from plants-
Application to waves and gulfs first will advance

But much more there is-or can be-simply just might
Inhabit the real, the imagined; far from sight

Though they be, the map has many uses beyond
Reaching *There*, knowing *Where*, and our crafter is fond

Of expression of wonders; illumination
Becomes he who harnesses his apperception

To illustrate what's across the hill or the sea.
So images swirl, though partisan it may be

To one who, likely, never the subjects has seen
Conceives deep-dwelling serpents, and beings obscene,

Animals out of lore, cataracts, swamps, and fires
Winds twelve in their number; his thoughts also may sire

Beings of holy writ; angels winged, looking down;
secular rumored rulers, bejeweled and crowned,

Even Prophet or God, if profane it is not
To adorn He, above, seeing all He has wrought.

If it follows purpose, the construct of the map,
And patrons receptive, if the real can adapt–

For those imagined entities, lands far away
Can be seen as invention, and viewer's minds stay

In the world of familiar. Cartographic skill
Is burgeoned by the study of other maps, stills

In disparate books, on skins of dimmer times than
Even the present, seemingly perceptive *When.*

Evolved peoples and instruments; distances shrunk
By the course of explorers and diligent monks,

Traders on the Silk Road, others vying for first
In the race to the Indies and its fragrant purse

In barks battered, triumphant; some lost to the waves–
Every traverse brought knowledge–and that done to stave

Off the dark of uncertainty. The map-maker,
hands placed now on his thighs, examines the acres,

The metes and the bounds, the leagues, rods, furlongs, and miles;
Checks notations and maps left by elders; compiles

And considers it all in his thoughts once again.
Energy pulses, and his Vision returns; then,

The quill into ebony plunges, and the light
From the oil-lamp burns brightly; so, guided by right

He returns to his work, on a surface akin
To his own, and comparably weak and as thin

As the hold that we have on the moment. At peace
In his worldview, he draws until efforts may cease.

And the map now is finished, the ink yet to dry;
Does he know to what hands that fair skin is to fly?

Ever ephemeral are the works of our hands,
Signature of a sovereign, depictions of lands.

Tales of myth, lustful circumstance, sojourns and wars,
And, if his map is true, it might outlive many scores

Of the others. But-the artist? His manuscript
Unattributed, he is lost; thus, we are stripped

Of the maker, but he endures, we can agree
In his manifestations of lands and of sea.

A reflection of Earth. It is simple. Yet, too,
There is much more to mapping the *Here* than we knew.

"Back Roads"

America: We love the line, the submission of the snaking river to the rip-rap
channel, to be put under the heel of the perpendicular bridge when its back
must be broken. Straighten it all out, make it right and true, the efficiency of
angles and the thirteen bars.
We are the transcontinentalists; sea to shining sea, damned whatever's in front.
Railway to highway-
cut, fill, tunnel, grind it, grade it, lay it out. And we'll square it,
wielding and cursing mathematics as we go,
and latitude and longitude will shrink to territories, states, counties, townships,
precincts, sections, quarters, acres and city blocks, sidewalks to backyards and
the assessed feet on a tax notice.
But as the eagle clasps both vine and victory, there's polarity in us,
one that has the spear-strength to drive another before it or pierce itself,
and every early light of dawn presents an opportunity for conflict, little civil
wars at the Shell or Walmart,
freedom of expression unencumbered by cares of old:
"To hell with laws; We don't walk the line."
Resistance rears, plots and plats go out the window and the snake's let loose
again,
squared signs shot and papers crushed for throwing.
There's a little hiding in us all, we Old-World border-breakers,
and nowhere does the rebel show more clearly than on the earthen roads,
scraped down and root-stripped and still alive, where you drive for just the
drive.
Oh, they fight the lines themselves, those county tracks that corral
both cattle and caretaker,
and though we demanded them as wagons and Fords broke ankles on the two-
tracks,
and though we'll swear and spit at washboards or unseen divot,
within us-windows open to reddening elbows-we approve,
for there's a mutiny: the self-reclamation of a road.

Heat-cracks in early August as the corn bows in its approval and dust-devils
dance, shaking even diesels when they partner,
rocks erupting after torrential rain-rains that incise the road as cartographers
onto copper plate,
washouts that remove almost all trace and leave it stalk-filled,
crushed culverts, the road's distaste for metal clear as when it creeps into the
cattle grates,
it seems to call the February drifts to hide them, for maybe we'll forget there
was a road there-
and ever does it gnaw its right-of-way, snapping at this side or that,
inviting signs to bend and sag and the grass and sedge to seed it back to health.

There's our grandfather, child of the Rail and carefree in his age,
and we as favored grandkids, rocking upon his lap as there's talk of "real work"
and those city people and miles of fenceposts, in his way giving sanction to the
breakdown of the rigid, and smiling as we leave those posts in the dust behind
us and search for curves.

"Mappamundi"

(On the *Psalter Map* of 1265)

See—the beyond, of the monsterous races, afar to the lands lying
Past our eyes, breathing, opaque but alive. And while different men of a more
Noble masque, confident, brand then efface, simply contrast those denizens
Who, in submission to lettered intelligence pure but still infantile,

Shamble and scrape on a barren plain. Further apart, duly walled in their
Wrath, both retained and retainers for hatred, the tearers paw; ruin lurks
Always at margins of mind.   For disturbance, division, anarchical
Magog and Gog, the infernal, stoke fires for consuming the truth-bearers.

Distant, though, England, on circling ocean, sits calmly at borders to
Known and to suspect. There, Portugal, France, and Castile; blest new Rome
with its
Latin still vibrant as erudites know, embraced *lingua* of ancients, of
Scholars, monastics bestowing, by quill, appellations of lore and real.

Washed, too, in feverish rumors of others and outlands, perhaps to the
North-obscured shadowy coastlines or forests viewed not through but
vap'rous grey,
Few, though, were scribes or were chronicling brothers who inked out the
boreal
Lands, and so "Ultima Thule" stayed whispered, an image in only thought.

All the while watches the Trinity-three beholds continents three-as the
Sphere of the world, incompletely but gently expressed, with a tethering
Center-Jerusalem-root of the tree, there to consecrate everything
Europe believed. Immature and unseasoned, of fancies and fits are they,

Seeking to know the foundations of God, how in radiance He formed the
Earth and its depths, the extent of which none of the learn'ed might say, nor
could
Place. Add the leagues, add the furlongs, untrodden, not sailed, from the
unpassaged
East did the spiritual, secular wealth lay beclouded in dimmest light.

Mountains and cataracts, freshets uncharted and raging, inhabitants
Sinful or sinned-less; and, somewhere, a towering height from which spills, to
the
Cast-aways, waters familiar whose hearts carve, in stone and soil, channels-the
Cross on the orb, the salvation of Man from intemperate, damning ills.

East, continental, which summits the map, reveals forfeited Paradise,
Earthen and tangible-flows of those muscular rivers do prove-yet its
Pinnacle out and afar, for in gaps nest chimerical terrors and
Doubts, and while arising sunrays the path they do light, only One may view.

Where, then, the occident? Lands to the west, contradictory, dim if not
Hollow and false. Oppositioned to theory, theology both, and though
Poets in lines sung of heroes and quests, those more grounded or fearful knew
Zephyrus whirled over Biblical mains, 'cross a singular, soundless sea;

Vastness familiar in heavens and mind, the imagined exclusively
Sanctioned when tied to the spiritual, psalmists assuaging and testaments
Dictative, regions beyond living eye, to be referenced, copied as
"Then" if not "there"; to exist while apart was to build upon rolling sands.

Minds, oh, shall wander, and mystery lived in conceptions of East. Shrouded
Africa, vague past its crest, with its dwellers alike and apart, whether
Diff'rent in shape or in soul, yet still given a humanoid outline and
Aspect. More dreamed on was high-centered India, veiled, and spiced to start

Urges, for gemstones, for gain, for a countenance splendid if fictile-but
Palpable, gilded, reflected by kings, all the riches of certainty
Mingled with wonder. Unknown was the route, nonetheless, to traverse, and
so
Orient only the parchment would show, undrawn occident left to doubt.

Thus, the Atlantic awaited, its nature unsure but tremendous; though
Barks still would navigate, margins to thin, with the resolute captains as
Surveyors, noting what is and what may, ever compassing more than the
Chart of the previous year, withal grasping known bound'ries as mooring
straps.

Landed septentrional, and Brazil, countless isles set affixed onto
Waters like aquamarine. Antipodeal lands inconceived, and from
Cloisters and courts undiscern'ed and still, the rever'sed uncircumvolved
Tri-grounded globe berthed no province, no contour illumined was placed at
sea.

Candle-light glist'ning before; the worn feather, tip resting, returned to its
Perch; precious colors, from ores and from sea-creatures scant, gently placed
into
Cabinets oak; his hands copper-stained ever to be, a name lost within
History's push, lives ephemeral, all to decay, save the parchment's trace.

Tilted stand, bearing skin, ink, flesh, and world; see the sphere now incarnate
for
Substantiation. The winds ring the ocean; encompassing not all, just
Three-while the Heavens and Trinity swirl. Speculation, or wonder, if
Present, lay still in the well, as breaths quickened in those of the setting sun.

"Instrument"

Abiding every space along our course,
no unchained acre, unknown shore without;
and seekers cry for it with voices hoarse
while pledging bodies, souls as the devout;
apparent to the face as rain, as winds
to flaccid sails awaiting, doldrum trapped,
its presence yet unseen to those of kin
divergent, eyes beholding other maps;
confounding as the shrouded night, no star
at pole or constellation bearing gives,
but one, to destination near or far,
magnetic pull will draw to where it lives.
Location of the endpoint will be found
If calibration of the heart is sound.

"Delimitation"

We walk apartment hallways, our destinations dull but settled,
past doorways leading into other worlds-worlds
of the same orbit but in tighter or wider circles, our rare conjunctions
not celebrated nor seen as portents now
and marked only by a nod or marginal remark.
And so it is as well upon concreted arterials, from avenues coiffed to
transit-pummeled city routes and urban highways
where we plot our simple course on lighted glass and wait for the commands,
or, more usually,
let mind and muscle memory create a current for us
as we sit as steerage inside our little ships,
en route but still adrift in parallel passage.
Even as we return to our adopted point of beginning, the start and end
of such and such a day,
a bedroom lined with images and symbols understood, gadgets responsive and
predictable, and lay ourselves at rest,
the strange theater of our dreams, whose juxtaposing scenes sometimes
confound,
sometimes entrance and leave us all too-wanting as we wake,
will often set us common figures and facades upon its stage,
and we, seeking comfort within an endless imagination, watch again
a familiar fiction.

But it is not always so inside that temple home,
and when we wonder, morning-struck, upon the reopening of eyes
of the vistas odd, curious faces that beckoned us to that beyond our view,
exotic and enigmatic, and think of them of something more than fancy,
it may be that an old desire had taken to the wheelhouse
and, momentarily, cast our chart aside.

And one may justly question if deferring to delineation,
the waypoints and landmarks of every other day, familiar stars above, signs
to guide us on already well worn-paths of lines and limitations,
becomes us:
Are we, when routine and regiment is left behind, so dissimilar
from those who set out to cross the limits of the known,
its girdling boundary of endless waters?
For were they not like us, too,
of wanting payments and responsibilities, chores of hearth
and frailty of the flesh-
and while doubly weighted with custom of the Crown and a still-dim Reason,
adream of other spheres and shorelines?
No doubt they, too, found heavy that straying step,
for we have battled for the Pause, the refuge of society,
and while the boldest may re-form the world
discovery is inked on maps in black as well as red.

It remains in us, the urge and the animation, but exploration
is not particular to latitude and longitude, nor must one surmount a peak or
chase the horizon;
it is only the passing of a boundary, the piercing of our own margins
by which the navigator and discoverer returns,
our courses are corrected-
and those akin from other simple worlds
will meet us then
to share what we have seen and dreamed.

About the Author

Brian P. Croft is an instructor of Composition and Literature and lives in the western United States. Research in history and cartography, and the study of nature through hiking and travel, comprise much of his time outside of the classroom, as does the writing of fiction, poetry, and personal essays. This is his first published collection of poems.

Printed in the USA
CPSIA information can be obtained
at www.ICGtesting.com
LVHW070723120924
790718LV00015B/91